-- NOV 2018

D1141464

Leabharlanna Poiblí Chathair Bhaile Átha Cliath
Dublin City Public Libraries

Ballymun Branch Tel: 8421890

Comhairle Cathrach
Bhaile Átha Cliath
Dublin City Council

Oversize .

Due Date	Due Date	Due Date

WHERE'S MY WELLY?

THE WORLD'S GREATEST MUSIC FESTIVAL CHALLENGE

MATT EVERITT & JIM STOTEN

Laurence King Publishing

Newport Folk Festival

The International Montreux Jazz Festival

The Woodstock Music & Art Fair

The Pilton Pop, Folk & Blues Festival

Monsters of Rock

The Reading Festival

Coachella Valley Music
and Arts Festival

Tomorrowland

South by Southwest Music Festival

Bestival

Pinkpop

The Glastonbury Festival of
Contemporary Performing Arts

JOHN PEEL

Someone who had a passion for all genres
of music, with a 40-year broadcasting career
that included discovering some of the acts
within these pages, was the late, great DJ
John Peel. He is a legend and was no stranger
to many of the festivals, so we've honoured
him here by hiding him in every picture.

Music sounds better when you hear it as part of a crowd: under the sky or under a tent, in a field and at a festival. The idea of people assembling to listen to music is as old as music itself. Festivals follow in a tradition of rocks being walloped together in caves, animal-skin drums being beaten round campfires, and cathedral choirs leading congregations, and we still gather together today to see the artists we love, to share our excitement and to witness musical moments that make history.

Starting in 1965 at Newport, US, and ending at Glastonbury, England, today, this book collates twelve of the greatest festivals of all time, and each chapter illustrates some of the most legendary bands and performances ever.

As a festival is usually an outdoor experience, there is a welly boot hidden in each picture for you to find, in amongst the mud, mayhem and music. Can you also spot the famous musicians and fans who have helped secure each festival's iconic status?

So pack your tent, dig out your waterproofs, prepare for some unimaginably bad toilets and enter The World's Greatest Music Festival Challenge!

HOLE

Coachella Valley Music and Arts Festival
Empire Polo Club, Indio, California, USA | 29-30 April 2006

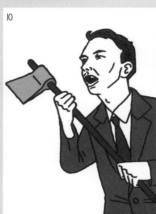

Newport Folk Festival

Newport, Rhode Island, US
22–25 July 1965

Some festivals are famous for specific moments, flashpoints that alter the course of music. The Newport Folk Festival of 1965 had one of those moments.

This is a story about Bob Dylan. We're not underplaying the significance of Newport as an event – from 1959 to 1970 it hosted the greatest names in folk, blues, gospel and country, including Joan Baez (1), The Kingston Trio (2), Pete Seeger, Odetta (3), Muddy Waters (4), Johnny Cash (5) and Howlin' Wolf (6) – but this is all about Dylan.

Dylan had played Newport twice before, as an acoustic act, and the crowd loved him. 'Blowin' in the Wind' and 'Mr. Tambourine Man' were already famous as hits for other people, and many at Newport saw this wild-haired young man as following in a tradition of classic protest singers like Woody Guthrie. On the Saturday of the event he had even taken part in a well-received song workshop, performing some of his best-known tunes.

However – and it's a big however – Dylan (7) took the stage on Sunday, accompanied by members of The Butterfield Blues Band (8), with a Fender Stratocaster. An electric guitar. He proceeded to stun the audience with three blistering, rackety and ear-pummellingly loud rock 'n' roll songs, with lyrics seemingly focused on the personal, not the political. There had been electric performances at Newport before, but none as ferocious as this; and, above all, no one expected such a performance from Dylan.

Legend says that the entire crowd turned hostile, jeering and booing, but the reality is hard to pin down. A proportion of the audience was certainly appalled by the show, and organizers and folk 'purists', including musicians such as Seeger and Ewan MacColl (9), were angry at this 'betrayal' of folk principles, both in terms of amplification but also because of Dylan's move away from the protest song format. Famously, Seeger (10) is said to have fetched an axe and tried to cut the PA cables (something that he later explained was prompted by his frustration at the distorted sound, which meant he couldn't hear Dylan's all-important lyrics).

Other witness reports differ enormously. Some say only journalists were heckling (the New York Times (11) later reported that Dylan 'was roundly booed by folk-song purists, who considered this innovation the worst sort of heresy'), while others recall the crowd enjoying the set. Yet more claim that any negative reaction was simply down to the shortness of Dylan's set – he was onstage for only 15 minutes.

None of this really matters. The event was legendary by the time Dylan walked off stage. For the wider music world, this was the point when folk broke with tradition and became amplified by aggression, and the moment that rock music lost its naivety and gained a more political and poetic agenda. You could hear this new attitude in music that followed by The Beatles (12), The Byrds (13) and The Rolling Stones (14). Neither folk nor rock would ever be the same again; it was the end of an era for both.

The International Montreux Jazz Festival

Montreux Casino (and nearby venues),
Lake Geneva, Montreux, Switzerland
18-22 June 1969

Montreux is the world's most famous jazz festival. It's based around a casino in a beautiful Swiss city reclining on the shores of Lake Geneva. But don't let the posh surroundings fool you. If you have passion for music, you're welcome.

The event is synonymous with Montreux local **Claude Nobs (1)**. He worked for the tourist office and enlisted jazz musician Géo Voumard and journalist René Langel to help him launch a world-class jazz festival in a city with no obvious connections to the genre (and thousands of miles from the American jazz heartlands). However, Nobs was an ambitious chap (he persuaded The Rolling Stones to play their first European show in Montreux in 1964), and his tenacity bore fruit with the first festival, in June 1967, a three-day event that included The **Charles Lloyd (2)** Quartet, featuring future jazz heroes Keith Jarrett and Jack DeJohnette.

By 1969 the event had expanded to five days and entered history. The bill that year included **Kenny Burrell (3)**, as well as **Les McCann and Eddie Harris (4)**, who recorded the million-selling album *Swiss Movement* at the show. The Casino Kursaal de Montreux played host to **Ella Fitzgerald (5)**, who performed a now legendary set that included songs by **Dusty Springfield**, **Cream** and **The Beatles (6)**, proving that she deserved her status as 'First Lady of Song'. That year Montreux also started a trend of embracing apparently opposing genres, opening its doors to progressive band Colosseum and rock outfit **Ten Years After (7)**.

The casino itself entered musical folklore after it famously burned down in 1971 during a performance by **Frank Zappa (8)**. According to myth, an audience member let off a flare gun and the resulting ball of flame became stuck in the rattan-covered ceiling. The fire spread quickly and destroyed the entire building, incinerating all of Frank Zappa's equipment (except, oddly, a cowbell), but miraculously no one was seriously hurt. **Deep Purple (9)** watched the blaze from the safety of their hotel across Lake Geneva, and wrote the rock classic 'Smoke on the Water' (1972) about the incident.

The casino was rebuilt in 1975 and the festival continued to grow, encompassing more eclectic musical forms as it did so. It is no surprise that such jazz greats as **Count Basie (10)**, **Miles Davis (11)**, **Etta James (12)**, **Quincy Jones (13)**, **Oscar Peterson (14)**, **Nina Simone (15)** and **Dizzy Gillespie (16)** all appeared, but no other jazz event can boast of visits from **James Brown (17)**, **Queen (18)**, **Outkast (19)**, **Leonard Cohen (20)**, **Prince (21)** (who in 2013 played four times in three days), **Ray Charles (22)**, **John Legend (23)**, **Mary J. Blige (24)**, **Massive Attack (25)** and **Marvin Gaye (26)**.

Nobs died in 2013, but he lived long enough to see his vision of attracting people to this small, picturesque city evolve into a two-week event drawing over 250,000 visitors. He made what was once called 'the Pearl of the Swiss Riviera' into one of the jewels in the crown of the music world.

The Woodstock Music & Art Fair

White Lake, Bethel, New York, US
15-18 August 1969

If you hear the words 'rock festival' and you think instantly of hippies, mud and Hendrix, then you're thinking about Woodstock, the defining music event of the 1960s and probably the most famous festival ever.

Its promoters, John Roberts, Joel Rosenman, Artie Kornfeld and Michael Lang (1), wanted to stage 'three days of music and peace' in the town of Woodstock, a popular hang-out for musicians such as Bob Dylan (2), but local wrangling shifted the event to a 240-hectare (600-acre) site some 80 kilometres (50 miles) away, owned by dairy farmer Max Yasgur (3). They secured an impressive line-up and sold over 100,000 tickets, but they also seriously underestimated how popular the festival would be. The entire area was swamped with music fans, who broke through the perimeter fences and turned Woodstock into a free event that was attended by an estimated half a million people.

Those who made it inside witnessed a staggering show. Following festival opener Richie Havens (4) were such soon-to-be-famous musicians as Santana (5) and Joe Cocker (6), international stars like Ravi Shankar (7), supergroups such as Crosby, Stills, Nash & Young (8) (playing only their second show) and career-defining sets from legendary artists like Sly & The Family Stone (9), Arlo Guthrie (10), Janis Joplin (11), The Who (12) and Country Joe and the Fish (13). Recordings tell us that not every set was a triumph (The Grateful Dead (14) acknowledged they played a stinker), but over the years nearly every performance has become iconic.

The best-known image from Woodstock (apart from crazy naked people) is Jimi Hendrix (15), resplendent in a fuchsia headband and white, tasselled jacket. Hendrix actually took to the stage at 9 o'clock on the Monday morning, and performed to a weary and depleted crowd of less than 200,000. However, his searing psychedelic rendition of 'The Star-Spangled Banner' became regarded as a statement against the Vietnam War and stands as a seminal moment in rock 'n' roll.

Music aside, in many ways Woodstock was a fiasco. There were food shortages, poor sanitation and a hell of a lot of mud, but the festival's reputation as a cosmic utopia has since been cemented by the slightly unreliable, psychedelic-tinged memories of the crowd, organizers and bands. However, the young audience - brought together by a mutual love of music and a rejection of the establishment that had started the war in Vietnam - functioned as a self-governing community, and the event succeeded (generally) thanks to their good intentions.

Woodstock left its promoters almost bankrupt, but the release in 1970 of a film about the festival (edited in part by Martin Scorsese (16)) helped to recoup their losses. More significantly, it captured the spirit of Woodstock and secured its status as a triumph for the countercultural ethos of peace and understanding.

Joni Mitchell (17), distraught at not being able to attend, wrote a song about the festival in which she described it as a place where people 'saw that they were part of a greater organism'. This might have sounded a little naive had she been talking about any other event, but in the case of Woodstock she was totally right.

The Pilton Pop, Folk & Blues Festival
Worthy Farm, Pilton, Somerset, UK
19–20 September 1970

This is when the legend was born: the very first Glastonbury Festival. Okay, it may have been a slightly shaky start, and there are precious few similarities between the festival's debut and its vast modern counterpart, but the story of the best-loved music festival in the world starts here.

In June 1970 the Somerset dairy farmer Michael Eavis (1) and his partner and future wife, the late Jean Eavis (2) (who would prove just as important in Glastonbury's future), gatecrashed the Bath Festival of Blues and Progressive Music. It featured Led Zeppelin (3) and Frank Zappa (4) among others, and was considered a huge success, prompting Eavis to organize his own festival later that year. Staged at his home, Worthy Farm in Pilton, Somerset, it began on Saturday 19 September 1970, the day after Jimi Hendrix (5) died – something that must have been 'a bummer' to the 1,500 hippies who attended. As for the line-up, The Kinks (6) were booked as headliners but didn't turn up, so Marc Bolan (7) of the hippie duo Tyrannosaurus Rex (later refashioned as glam pop outfit T. Rex) was enlisted as a replacement. Eavis remembers Bolan arriving in a velvet-covered car – cool, but staggeringly impractical for a dairy farm. Festival-goers paid £1 entrance and everyone got free milk, while just 30 stewards oversaw the slightly dodgy infrastructure and eye-watering toilet facilities. It was a ramshackle and good-natured affair, drawing the attention of a BBC film crew (8).

In terms of entertainment, as well as Bolan you would have seen Quintessence, Stackridge, Al Stewart, Ian Anderson (9), Keith Christmas (10), Amazing Blondel, Sam Apple Pie, plenty of cows and the brilliantly named DJ Mad Mick (11), who described the event thus: 'It was like an English country fête, with longer hair and no cream teas.' The late, great DJ John Peel (12) was there too (we will cross paths with him more than once on our festival journey), and in fact a Glasto stage was renamed in his honour in 2004.

The whole town of Glastonbury is steeped in mystical history, and that permeates the festival site. The grave of King Arthur (13) is supposedly at Glastonbury Abbey, legends abound of Merlin the Wizard (14) visiting the area, and some believe the Holy Grail is buried at the foot of Glastonbury Tor (15). The festival itself is said to be situated on a meeting point of ley lines – the mysterious prehistoric pathways that some claim crisscross the UK – and Stonehenge (16) isn't far away. This all means that there's an undeniably magical atmosphere at Glastonbury. Who knows whether that's down to the cosmic vibes of the earth, the ghosts of ancient Avalon or just the local cider?

Amazingly, from these humble beginnings today's record-breaking annual Glastonbury Festival was born. The event was larger the next year, in 1971; Arthur Brown (17), Hawkwind (18) and David Bowie (19) all performed, and Eavis constructed the event's first iconic Pyramid Stage.

But this is where it all began ....

Monsters of Rock
Castle Donington, Leicestershire, UK
22 August 1981

Denim and leather - as the band Saxon pointed out - can bring us together, and the Monsters of Rock Festival was where those two sartorial elements were showcased in their natural habitat: in the mud, in the English Midlands and in the midst of deafening music.

From 1980 to 1996 Monsters of Rock was the biggest and best heavy rock festival in the world - and when I say 'rock', I mean the kind of tight-trousered, long-haired rock that turns its amplifiers up to 11 and head-bangs till dawn.

There were two major reasons for its success. First, it was staged in the Midlands, the birthplace and spiritual home of metal. Black Sabbath (1), (half of) Led Zeppelin (2), Slade (3) and Judas Priest (4) all hail from the region, and the honesty, power and humour in the music struck a chord with the unpretentious Midlands temperament. Secondly, metal fans are fiercely loyal, so elder statesmen like Alice Cooper (5), Ozzy Osbourne (6) and Hawkwind (7) were welcomed with throaty roars of approval alongside upcoming bands such as Def Leppard (8), Diamond Head and the aforementioned Saxon (9).

The second Monsters of Rock festival in 1981 featured the hugely loved Radio 1 rock DJ Tommy Vance (10) as host, heritage act Blue Öyster Cult (11), '80s rock heroes Whitesnake (12), glam survivors Slade and the already legendary AC/DC (13).

It also ticked a lot of the archetypal festival boxes: a distinctly unglamorous site (a motor-racing circuit); shockingly basic toilets; and a vast, sweaty, greasy, long-haired, drunken rabble of a crowd. They were a generally happy bunch, but rowdy and definitely mischievous, and that brings us to an unavoidable Monsters of Rock tradition. However fantastic the line-up or beloved the compère, if you were in the audience, at some point it would be your avowed duty to throw something at the stage: food, rubbish, paper aeroplanes, the always-popular toilet rolls and, most frequently, plastic beer bottles. Occasionally empty, but more often than not full (and rarely of beer ... if you catch my drift). And that's what the audience did to bands they *liked*.

Over the years Monsters of Rock would attract icons such as Metallica (14), Motörhead (15), Guns N' Roses (16), Aerosmith (17), ZZ Top (18), Meat Loaf (19), Bon Jovi (20), Iron Maiden (21) and KISS (22) before the genre dipped in popularity, thanks in part to the wave of grunge bands who rejected the flamboyance and spectacle of metal. The last Monsters of Rock event was staged in 1996.

One-off Monsters of Rock festivals crop up occasionally in various countries, and the Castle Donington site that hosted the original event for 16 years is now the home of the annual Download Festival, which showcases (yes, you guessed it) heavy metal from around the world. More to the point, you can still find many of the bands that played the festival in the 1980s on both festivals' bills today - a sure sign that Monsters of Rock really was the greatest metal music Mecca.

The Reading Festival
Richfield Avenue, Reading, Berkshire, UK
28–30 August 1992

The Reading Festival has been a jazz event, a hippy haven, a showcase for punk and a temple to heavy metal, but in 1992 the indie music scenes of the USA and UK met on a bill topped by a band that would bring the underground into the mainstream.

The festival can be traced back to 1961 and the National Jazz and Blues Festival in Richmond, Surrey. It shifted location throughout the 1960s before focusing on rock acts like **The Rolling Stones (1)**, **Pink Floyd (2)** and **Cream (3)**, and eventually found its current home in 1971.

As the 1970s became the 1980s, punk and new wave bands including **The Jam (4)**, **The Cure (5)** and **The Police (6)** appeared, as well as heavy rock bands like **Thin Lizzy (7)** and **Status Quo (8)**. However, by 1992 the line-up was a mix of established UK indie bands like **The Wonder Stuff (9)** and **The Charlatans (10)**, hip-hop from **Public Enemy (11)** and **Beastie Boys (12)**, and a new generation of British bands such as **Suede (13)**, **Manic Street Preachers (14)** and **PJ Harvey (15)**, who were setting the scene for Britpop.

But 1992 meant grunge. Nirvana had played low on the bill the previous year, but in the wake of their album *Nevermind* and single 'Smells Like Teen Spirit', they returned to headline as the most important band on the planet. Singer **Kurt Cobain (16)** picked the Sunday bill himself, choosing fellow US grunge acts **Mudhoney (17)**, **L7 (18)** and, bizarrely, ABBA (19) tribute band **Björn Again (20)**, among others.

In the days leading up to Nirvana's appearance, rumours swirled backstage: 'Had Kurt overdosed?' 'Had his wife, **Courtney Love (21)**, overdosed?' 'Was the band going to play at all?'

Eventually the lights went down and Kurt emerged, pushed onstage in a wheelchair dressed in a white surgical gown and wearing a long blonde wig (to make him look like Love, who had just had their baby). 'He'll pull through,' Nirvana's bassist **Krist Novoselic (22)** told the half-concerned, half-amused audience. Cobain pulled himself up to the microphone, sang one line of a **Bette Midler (23)** ballad and collapsed. It was, of course, a stunt. Moments later Nirvana (who drummer **Dave Grohl (24)** subsequently admitted were seriously under-rehearsed) bludgeoned through a set that has gone down in history as one of the most powerful festival shows ever, one they ended by trashing their equipment and leaving the stage in a squall of feedback noise. It was their last ever UK gig.

Reading survives and thrives to this day, and in 1999 it expanded to a sister site in Leeds. Grohl has headlined three times with **Foo Fighters (25)**, and virtually every major band has appeared. **Muse (26)**, **Arctic Monkeys (27)** and **Eminem (28)** have all played stormers, while the more famous failures include an out-of-tune appearance by **The Stone Roses (29)** in 1996, in a set described occasionally as 'the worst gig of all time'.

These days boutique 'experiential' festivals offer theatre, exotic food and cocktails. You won't find that at Reading. Its success proves that you don't need ley lines, interpretive dance collectives or Goan fish curry; sometimes all you need is a grubby field, gallons of booze and great bands.

1

2/3

14

5

6

7/8

12

10

11

9

13

14

16/17

18

15

Coachella Valley Music and Arts Festival
Empire Polo Club, Indio, California, US
29-30 April 2006

Coachella is perhaps the greatest of the modern music festivals. It took the best elements from festival history - impressive scale, eclectic line-ups, boutique amenities, beautiful surroundings and an eye on emerging trends - and staged them in the hugely efficient, highly profitable and massively impressive way that Americans do so well.

Pearl Jam (1) played the first gig at the Empire Polo Club in November 1993, using the location as an alternative to corporate-run music venues. Paul Tollett (2) and his business partner, the late Rick Van Santen (3), booked the show and recognized the potential of the site, and six years later they staged the first Coachella. It featured 70 acts (including Beck (4), Tool (5) and Rage Against the Machine (6)), but ran at a staggering $800,000 loss. Undeterred, Tollett and Van Santen tried again and again, refining their plans every year.

Coachella has grown to become a central part of the American music scene, drawing massive acts including Drake (7), The Weeknd (8), Radiohead (9), Arcade Fire (10) and LCD Soundsystem (11). It's also a place for bands to reunite, and Pixies (12), Siouxsie & The Banshees (13), The Jesus and Mary Chain (14) and Faith No More (15) all included Coachella in their reunion plans. Inevitably it's *the* destination for fashionistas and hip film stars, and currently the most profitable music festival in the USA - in 2015 it made just over $84 million from around 200,000 tickets.

But one Coachella performance has passed into legend. In 2005 Daft Punk had released their third album, *Human After All*, to mixed reviews. The elusive French duo of Thomas Bangalter (16) and Guy-Manuel de Homem-Christo (17) had not appeared live since 2001, and the once-groundbreaking duo seemed to be artistically static. But when Coachella lured them on to the bill in 2006 with a reported $300,000, they plunged the fee into creating a revolutionary stage show.

Clad in their trademark robot helmets and matching leather jumpsuits, the pair took to the stage in the dance tent to the strains of the *Close Encounters* theme, and embarked on a brilliantly crafted mix of their three albums, backed by jaw-dropping visual effects. 'The Robots' stood under the apex of a huge pyramid, while massive banks of LEDs and a colossal lighting rig were gradually revealed, the scale and intensity of the graphic projections, lights and lasers growing with every song. Many of the crowd recorded the performance on their phones, so that soon millions had watched a gig that proved electronic music could match the power, spectacle and impact of a traditional live band. This was the moment live dance took on rock, and won.

The set secured Daft Punk's status as icons and effectively kicked off the EDM (Electronic Dance Music) movement in the States, dragging dance music from the margins to become a major mainstream concern. Now electronic acts can be found topping the bills of festivals around the world and, for America at least, this moment was lift off.

Incidentally, Madonna (18) also played Coachella that year. But compared to Daft Punk, no one seemed that bothered.

Tomorrowland
De Schorre, Boom, Belgium
27–29 July 2012

Tomorrowland proves, in spectacular style, that dance music can attract audiences just as large and over-excitable as those for any rock band. Taking place in the aptly named Belgian town of Boom, it's a mind-blowingly vast three-day (and night) party that's basically Disneyland for ravers.

The journey from serious experimental electronic music pioneers, such as **Kraftwerk (1)**, **Can (2)** and **Tangerine Dream (3)** in the 1960s and 1970s, to a frankly bananas event like Tomorrowland is rather complicated. In the wake of disco (and such seminal tracks as 'I Feel Love' by **Giorgio Moroder (4)** and **Donna Summer (5)**), the 1980s brought tunes like 'Planet Rock' by **Afrika Bambaataa (6)**, and DJs such as New York's **Larry Levan (7)** and Chicago's **Frankie Knuckles (8)**. They laid the groundwork for the acid house movement that hurled dance music into the charts and inspired the (often illegal) raves where DJs spun tunes to huge, wide-eyed crowds.

For a long time **Jean-Michel Jarre (9)** was the only electronic artist who could attract serious audiences, but in the 1990s DJs began to evolve into superstars, among them **Fatboy Slim (10)**, **Carl Cox (11)**, **Sasha (12)** and **Pete Tong (13)**. Along with chart fixtures like **Moby (14)**, **Underworld (15)** and **Daft Punk (16)**, they took dance music from the clubs to the stadiums. And after a stadium, where can you go? A festival, obviously.

Tomorrowland first took place in 2005, when it attracted about 10,000 dance-music fanatics. Helped by the popularity of newer stars such as **Skrillex (17)**, **David Guetta (18)** and deadmau5, it grew to become a colossal annual event, attracting clubbers from all over the world (attendance peaked in 2014 with a staggering 360,000), enjoying all types of electronic music, including electro, trance, house, rave, drum & bass, hardcore, gabber, dubstep, hi-NRG and hundreds of confusing subgenres.

Now, most DJs are remarkably skilled at choosing incredible tracks, building atmosphere and creating a euphoric vibe, but visually it's just someone standing behind some hi-fi equipment. To combat this potentially rather dull experience, the organizers of Tomorrowland create the biggest spectacle possible. Fans enter a mystical world filled with vast, themed stage sets, elaborately costumed dancers and funfairs, and the DJ sets are accompanied by glitter cannon, smoke bombs, streamers, strobes, lasers and truly insane numbers of fireworks. In 2012 the festival boasted a stage that resembled a fantasy bookshelf with a library of gigantic fairy-tale books 28 metres (92 feet) high. All this plus some of the biggest names in dance music, including **Swedish House Mafia (19)**, Afrojack, **Calvin Harris (20)**, **Dimitri Vegas & Like Mike (21)**, **Pendulum (22)**, **Nervo (23)**, Richie Hawtin aka Plastikman, **Sven Väth (24)**, **Armin van Buuren (25)**, **The Bloody Beetroots (26)**, **Tiësto (27)**, **Steve Aoki (28)** and **Avicii (29)**.

So, yes, it's taken a while for dance-music festivals to match the scale of rock events, but for sheer spectacle Tomorrowland is the biggest party in the world. Heaven knows what Kraftwerk would make of it.

South by Southwest Music Festival
Various venues, Austin, Texas, US
12–17 March 2013

Just because you're a festival, it doesn't mean you have to be in a field, and South by Southwest is an urban music event that is just as popular, exciting and influential as any pastoral gathering.

SXSW started as a small, local music-business conference in 1987, and soon became an annual event. As word spread, bands came from further afield, and music biz types (and, importantly, non-business music fans) eager to check out hotly tipped, undiscovered groups started to congregate in the city.

Texas has been home to such country music heroes as **Willie Nelson (1)**, Bob Wills and **Kenny Rogers (2)**, but the cliché of the Lone Star State just being full of cowboys and truck drivers isn't true. Artists as varied as **Buddy Holly, Roy Orbison, Janis Joplin (3), Sly Stone (4)** and **Beyoncé (5)** all hail from Texas, and Austin prides itself on being a broad-minded place. Locals have a non-corporate mindset and are fiercely proud of their eclectic music and counterculture scene. There's a good reason why some Austinites adopted the unofficial slogan 'Keep Austin Weird'.

By 2013 SXSW was showcasing more than 2,000 artists over 113 venues and stages, the keynote speaker was **Dave Grohl (6)** and *USA Today* described the event as one of the 'largest and most influential gatherings on the planet'.

It's also *the* place to be discovered. The festival has served as a launch pad for the careers of **John Mayer (7)**, **Amy Winehouse (8)** and **James Blunt (9)** (the last of whom played to just 15 people in 2003 but was offered a US record deal on the spot). Florence Welch of **Florence + The Machine (10)** dived into an ornamental pond during her show in a Mexican restaurant in 2008, which helped to cement her live reputation.

Where there are big audiences, there's big business. As the event grew, so did the amount of company sponsorship, advertising and branded shows, and that hasn't gone down well with diehard fans. Likewise, established acts such as **Pharrell Williams (11)**, **Justin Timberlake (12)**, **The Flaming Lips (13)**, **Yeah Yeah Yeahs (14)** and **Snoop Dogg (15)** realized that SXSW is the perfect place to launch a new album or play a promotional corporate gig (or, in the case of **Lady Gaga (16)**, let a performance artist vomit green paint all over you before riding a mechanical bull. That actually happened).

Despite all this, SXSW has kept its soul. It remains the place where you could have seen acts like Haim, Chance The Rapper or alt-J before they became stars. More to the point, most fans can withstand oversubscribed shows and advertising if it means getting to see **Green Day (17)** or legends such as **Iggy and the Stooges (18)** or **Prince (19)** play rare intimate shows.

If anything illustrates how important SXSW is, in 2016 the SXSW Interactive Keynote speech was given by **President Barack Obama (20)**. While it's not known if he ended up chugging down the beers and stage-diving at Stubb's BBQ, this tells you that for six days every March, Austin, Texas, is the epicentre of the music world. And there's not a tent in sight.

Bestival

Robin Hill Country Park, Isle of Wight, UK
5–8 September 2013

If Bestival stands for anything, it's fun. Every September from 2004 till 2016, Robin Hill Country Park became a huge grown-up playground, complete with funfairs, fabulous discos, secret stages and 60,000 party people – most of whom appeared to have dived into a gigantic dressing-up box.

It was the brainchild of DJ **Rob da Bank (1)** and his wife, **Josie (2)**, who expanded the ethos of their hugely loved club nights and Sunday Best record label into a four-day bash on the Isle of Wight in the English Channel. That ethos was one of musical eclecticism, a freestyle, independent attitude and the love of a good party. And that's what Bestival is all about.

The first event featured **The Bees (3)**, **Basement Jaxx (4)**, **Lee 'Scratch' Perry (5)** and **Fatboy Slim (6)** playing for 10,000 people. By the tenth festival, the audience had quintupled, and there were nearly 60 stages, tents and stalls for music and daftness. Previous headliners included **Pet Shop Boys (7)**, **Beastie Boys (8)**, Amy Winehouse, **Dizzee Rascal (9)** and **Björk (10)**, but in 2013 the organizers pulled out the big guns in the shape of **Snoop Dogg (11)** and (playing his first major UK festival show) **Sir Elton John (12)** – who had such a good time that he jumped on top of his piano during his set. Other famous visitors to the site over the years have included **Howard Marks (13)**, **John Cooper Clarke (14)**, **Katy B (15)**, **Sean Paul (16)**, **Nile Rodgers (17)**, **Johnny Marr (18)** and **Ghostpoet (19)**.

Bestival also likes a big statement. Over the years it has housed the world's largest glitter ball (10.33 metres/34 feet across) and biggest bouncy castle (apparently taller than the Great Wall of China). In 2013 a full-size ship (the HMS *Bestival*) was used as a stage, and people flocked to pay their respects to a giant inflatable model of **Lionel Richie**'s head **(20)**.

You can't have Bestival without fancy dress, and every year it's different. Past themes have included 'Out of Space', 'Wildlife', 'Desert Island Disco' and 'Rock Stars, Pop Stars and Divas'. People take it very seriously: an amazing 55,000 people wore fancy dress in 2010, setting a new Guinness World Record.

In 2013 the theme was 'Nautical', and tens of thousands of aquatic characters took part in the traditional Saturday afternoon parade. Deep-sea divers, penguins, stingrays, someone dressed as a lighthouse and a less-than-regal-looking Neptune all joined circus performers dressed as pirates, Spanish galleon floats and mermaid acrobats. One witty festival-goer even dressed as the footballer **David Seaman (21)**.

Bestival is often said to be the first 'boutique' festival, and it broke the traditional festival mould by offering gourmet food, hot tubs, saunas, the opportunity to stay in luxury tepees, and special spaces for mums and kids (e.g. Breastival, an on-site yurt designated for breastfeeding). What's amazing is that, even now, when the event attracts 60,000 people (and has moved to Lulworth Castle in Dorset), it manages to keep that special atmosphere. It still feels as though all the grown-ups have disappeared and left the kids in charge of a festival on an enchanted island. So if you fancy spending three days wearing a dolphin onesie, this is the place for you.

Pinkpop
Megaland, Landgraaf, The Netherlands
10-12 June 2016

The first Pinkpop was organized by Jan Smeets (1) in 1970, and the gathering has taken place every single year since. This makes it the oldest continuous pop festival, not only in the Netherlands but also (it claims) in the world.

The inaugural event was staged at Burgemeester Damen Sportpark in Geleen on the Monday of Pentecost weekend (seven weeks after Easter Sunday in the Christian calendar), and the name Pinkpop derives from the Dutch word *Pinksteren*, meaning Pentecost. Organizers charged the equivalent of €1 a ticket to the 10,000 who attended, and the line-up featured Dutch bands like pop outfit George Baker Selection (2), psychedelic group De Dream, Livin' Blues (3) and rockers Golden Earring (4), as well as British Woodstock alumnus Keef Hartley (5).

As a one-day festival, it was soon attracting acts on the scale of Fleetwood Mac (6), Jeff Beck (7), Captain Beefheart (8) and Tom Petty and The Heartbreakers (9). It's also worth noting that John Peel (10) compèred every year from 1978 to 1986, and even had a stage named after him. Many big outdoor events floundered in the 1980s, but Pinkpop kept its ticket sales high and its audiences happy with bills that included The Specials (11), Lou Reed (12), Pixies (13) and Elvis Costello (14).

In the mid 1990s Pinkpop expanded into a multi-day bash at its current home of Megaland in Landgraaf, and by the mid 2000s its status as a premier-league festival was undeniable. Green Day (15), The Police (16), R.E.M. (17), The Rolling Stones (18), Kings of Leon (19) and U2 (20) all made Pinkpop a priority in their touring schedules.

The name 'Pinkpop' itself looms large across the site. It's impossible to avoid the colour pink, which is everywhere from stage awnings, tents and T-shirts to people's hair, face paint, feather boas and the traditional Pinkpop hats.

Pinkpop also has a reputation for attracting extremely enthusiastic fans. The Dutch for 'visitors' is *bezoekers*, and berserkers is a good description for many of the crowd. While the atmosphere on-site and in the camping area is calm and laid-back, the crowd can be utterly manic. Reports claim that during a set by Primus (21) in 1998 the impact of the audience jumping up and down registered over 1.0 on the Richter scale, and seething mosh pits are a common sight. That's not to say that the bands don't do their part: diving off the stage has become a sport for musicians at Pinkpop. In 1992 Eddie Vedder (22) climbed aboard a TV crane during his Pearl Jam (23) performance and did a breathtaking dive several metres into the throng. Similarly, if a group is having a good time onstage, they might just keep playing. When Bruce Springsteen (24) played his first ever European festival in 2009, he chose Pinkpop and performed an epic 24-song set that lasted nearly three hours.

It's hard to keep a festival going every year for more than four decades, but Pinkpop has managed it. Now more than 40 bands play each year, and since 1970 an incredible 2.3 million ticket holders have passed through the gates to enjoy one of the most relaxed and chaotic big-name festivals in the world. Think chilled! Think crazy! Think pink!

The Glastonbury Festival of Contemporary Performing Arts
Worthy Farm, Pilton, Somerset, UK
Last weekend of June

Since the Pilton Pop, Folk & Blues Festival launched in 1970, Glastonbury has grown to become the most eclectic, bizarre, exciting, inclusive and fun festival in the world, attracting legendary musicians and a huge, devoted audience.

It's now held on a 365-hectare (900-acre) site with a 14-kilometre (8.5-mile) perimeter fence, and plays host to about 175,000 festival-goers, musicians and site workers. These days some 3,000 acts perform around a galaxy of more than 100 stages, tents, bars, discos, circuses, cinemas, puppet theatres, political debates and all-night sound systems spiralling across the fields of Pilton, with the iconic Pyramid Stage at its heart.

Michael Eavis's (1) daughter Emily Eavis (2) now helps to run the event, and together they keep the spirit of the original Glastonbury alive. Glasto is the place where you can leave the normal world behind for a few days and immerse yourself in anti-establishment ideals of personal freedom, cooperation, environmentalism and tolerance.

Just as the surrounding landscape is steeped in the myths of Arthurian legend, so Glasto has myths of its own that circulate each year. Does the lost property department still have an unclaimed false leg? Did Prince (3) agree to headline, 'But only in May'? Did the lasers during the show by Orbital (4) blind a 747 pilot flying overhead? Has Lady Gaga (5) gone onstage wearing a dress made of bubbles? Was that Prince Charles (6) wandering across the Pyramid Stage? Did the Dalai Lama (7) give a speech at the Peace Garden? Will Radiohead (8), Pulp (9) or The Libertines (10) play unannounced surprise sets? Did Banksy (11) re-create Stonehenge out of chemical toilets somewhere on site? Did Michael Jackson (12) really die just as the festival started? (For the record, only one of those *didn't* happen.)

Then there are the bands. The biggest and greatest live acts in the world have headlined, including David Bowie (13), The Prodigy (14), Oasis (15), Blur (16) (twice), Coldplay (17) (four times), Jay Z (18), Florence + The Machine (19), The White Stripes (20), Paul McCartney (21), Muse (22) (three times), Arctic Monkeys (23), Fatboy Slim (24), Bruce Springsteen (25), Stevie Wonder (26), Beyoncé (27), Metallica (28), Arcade Fire (29), Kanye West (30), The Rolling Stones (31), The Smiths (32) and Adele (33). And that's barely scratching the surface. They all realize that Glasto crowds are some of the most passionate and dedicated around (tickets always sell out before a single act is confirmed), and a headlining set can be a career-defining moment.

But Glastonbury is all about the audience. Over the years millions of music fans have made Worthy Farm their home for a weekend, and there are a million Glastonbury stories: tales of campfire laughter, cosmic coincidences at the Stone Circle, late-night lunatic adventures, new friends and face-paint tomfoolery, impromptu marriages and misplaced minds, flooded tents and more than a few lost wellies. But rather than me trying to capture a moment of Glastonbury magic, I suggest that you try to get a ticket and experience it for yourself.

Published in 2018 by
Laurence King Publishing Ltd
361-373 City Road
London ECIV ILR
Tel +44 20 7841 6900
Fax +44 20 7841 6910
enquiries@laurenceking.com
www.laurenceking.com

A catalogue record for this book
is available from the British Library.

ISBN: 978 1 78067 977 8

Printed in China

Design: Alexandre Coco

ACKNOWLEDGEMENTS

MATT: I'd like to thank ... Jim for his amazing artistic
skills and staggering patience; Michael and Emily Eavis
and Nick Dewey for use of their logo and for inviting
everyone round each year; Rob and Josie da Bank; All at
LD Communications, The Outside Organisation, JMSPR,
Broadwick Live, Melvin Benn and Festival Republic, Live
Nation, Dawbell and AEG Live for letting me in; BBC
6 Music (esp Shaun), Radio 2 and Xfm for giving me a
professional reason to be there; Tam, Kwiss, Famous,
Andy W, Oli and Dave (B and W) for being first through
the gates back in the day; Menswear; The Montrose
Avenue; Mum, Roge, Dad, Joy, Alfie, and everyone who
ever got me in or out of trouble in a field; The frankly
brilliant Kate Haldane and all at PBJ; A very special
thanks to Camilla Morton, Alice Graham, Melissa Danny,
Alexandre Coco, Laurence himself and everyone at
Laurence King for making this happen; And Beth and
Joseph for being the best festival companions ever.

JIM: I'd like to thank Matt Everitt, Andrew Rae, Chrissie
Macdonald (and Rita), Camilla Morton, Melissa Danny,
Ma, Pa and Smelly, Jasper, Tom, Stethe, Dathe, Ben,
Tim, Dr Tom, Abbles, Faye, Indi, Billy Doctor, Guido,
Mariolina and Irene.